Bullfrog Books

Animals on the Farm

Sheep

by Wendy Strobel Dieker

Ideas for Parents and Teachers

Bullfrog Books give children practice reading informational text at the earliest levels. Repetition, familiar words, and photos support early readers.

Before Reading

- Discuss the cover photo with the class. What does it tell them?
- Look at the picture glossary together. Read and discuss the words.

Read the Book

- "Walk" through the book and look at the photos. Let the child ask questions.
- Read the book to the child, or have him or her read independently.

After Reading

- Prompt the child to think more. Ask: Would you like to have a sheep? Why or why not? Would you like to wear some wool mittens in winter?

Bullfrog Books are published by Jump!
5357 Penn Avenue South
Minneapolis, MN 55419
www.jumplibrary.com

Library of Congress Cataloging-in-Publication Data
Dieker, Wendy Strobel.
  Sheep / by Wendy Strobel Dieker.
    p. cm. -- (Bullfrog books: animals on the farm)
  Includes index.
  Summary: "Sheep narrate this photo-illustrated book describing the body parts and behavior of sheep on a farm. Includes photo glossary"--Provided by publisher.
  ISBN 978-1-62031-006-9 (hardcover)
  1. Sheep--Juvenile literature. 2. Sheep--Behavior--Juvenile literature. I. Title.
  SF375.2.D54 2013
  636.3--dc23
                            2012008424

Series Editor: Rebecca Glaser
Series Designer: Ellen Huber
Production: Chelsey Luther

Photo Credits: Alamy, 9, 12–13, 14–15, 23bl, 23br; Dreamstime, 7, 22 (inset); Getty, 5, 10, 16–17, 20-21, 23tr; National Geographic Stock, 18, 23tl; Shutterstock, 1, 3 (all), 6–7, 10–11, 13, 17, 22, 23ml, 23mr, 24; Superstock, 4, 8, 18-19

Printed in the United States of America at Corporate Graphics in North Mankato, Minnesota
7-2012/ PO 1121
10 9 8 7 6 5 4 3 2 1

Table of Contents

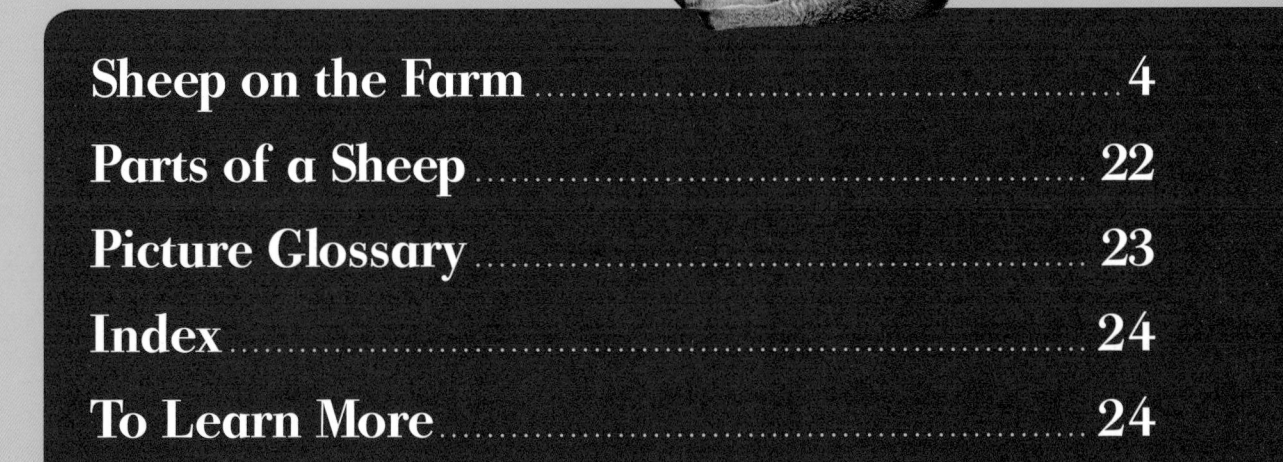

Sheep on the Farm 4

Parts of a Sheep 22

Picture Glossary 23

Index 24

To Learn More 24

Sheep on the Farm

I am a sheep.
I live on a farm.

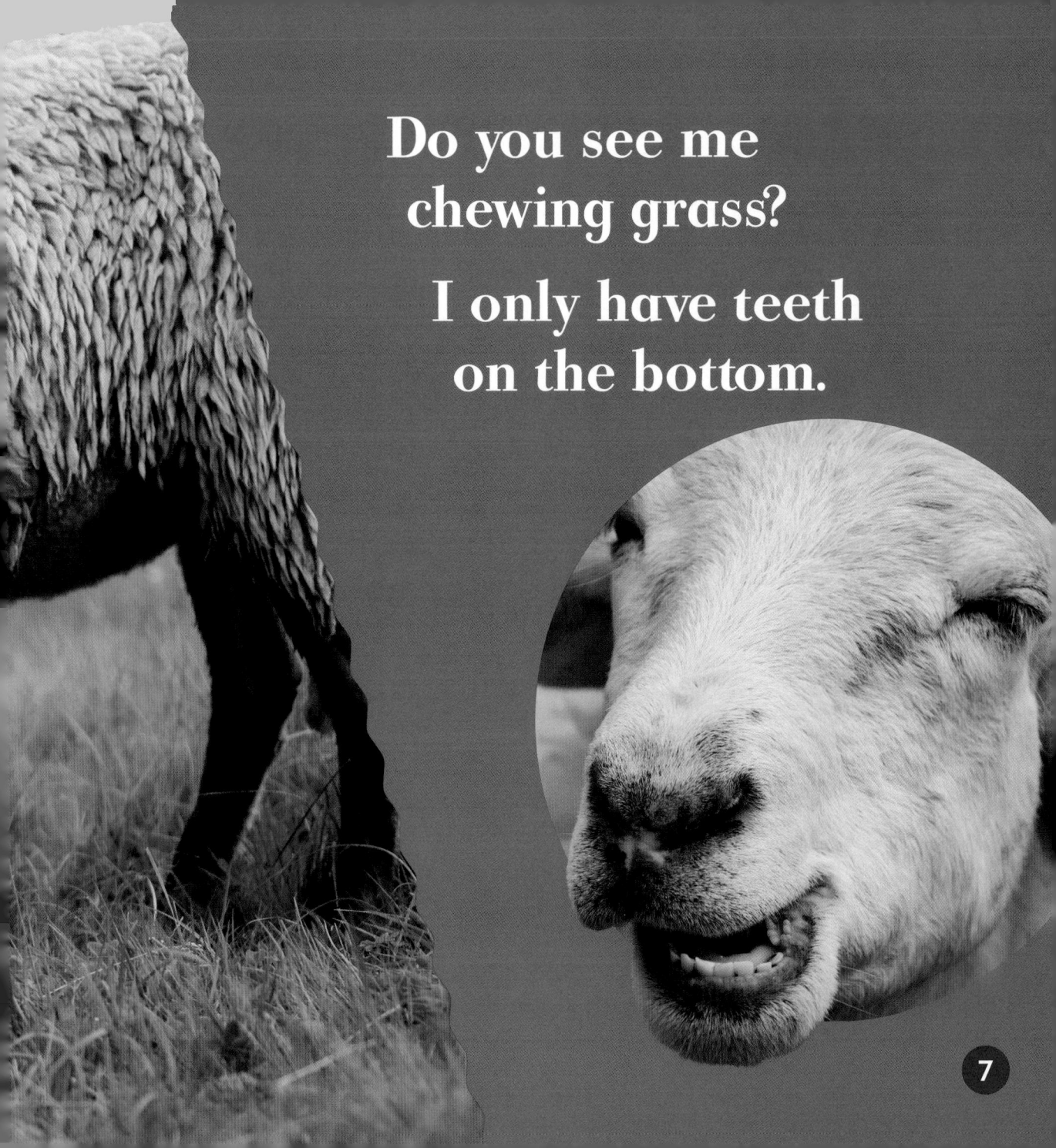

Do you see me chewing grass?

I only have teeth on the bottom.

Do you see my wool? It feels oily.

Wool keeps me dry and warm.

9

Do you see the farmer?
He cuts off my wool
in the spring.

Do you see the fleece?
It is one big
piece of wool.

Do you see
his horns?

A ram will fight
with his horns.

The farmer
keeps him in
his own pen.

ewe

Do you see
my flock?

Ewes and
their lambs
stay together.

lamb

bleat

Do you hear me bleat?
My lambs hear my voice.
They find me in the flock.

18

Here comes
the sheepdog!

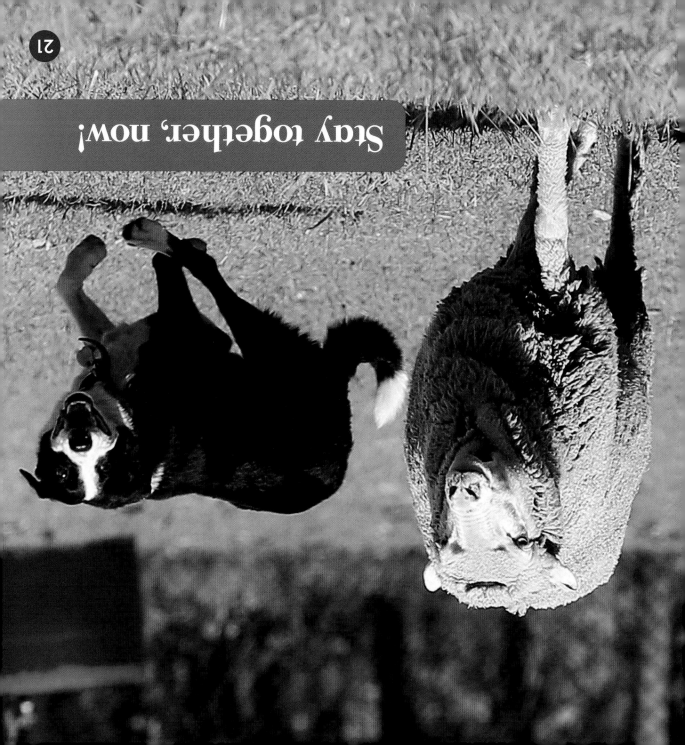

Stay together, now!

Parts of a Sheep

hoof
The hard outer covering of a sheep's foot.

teeth
White, bony parts in the mouth used to chew. Sheep only have teeth on the bottom.

wool
The soft, thick, curly hair of sheep.

horn
A hard, bony growth on the head.

Picture Glossary

bleat
The noise a sheep makes; it sounds like "baa."

ewe
A female sheep.

fleece
A big piece of wool that a farmer cuts off the sheep.

flock
A group of sheep that live together.

lamb
A baby sheep.

ram
A male sheep.

Index

bleat 18

ewes 17

farm 5

farmers 10, 14

fleece 13

flocks 17, 18

grass 7

horns 14

lambs 17, 18

rams 14

sheepdog 20

teeth 7

wool 8, 9, 10, 13

To Learn More

Learning more is as easy as 1, 2, 3.

1) Go to www.factsurfer.com

2) Enter "sheep" into the search box.

3) Click the "Surf" button to see a list of websites.

With factsurfer.com, finding more information is just a click away.